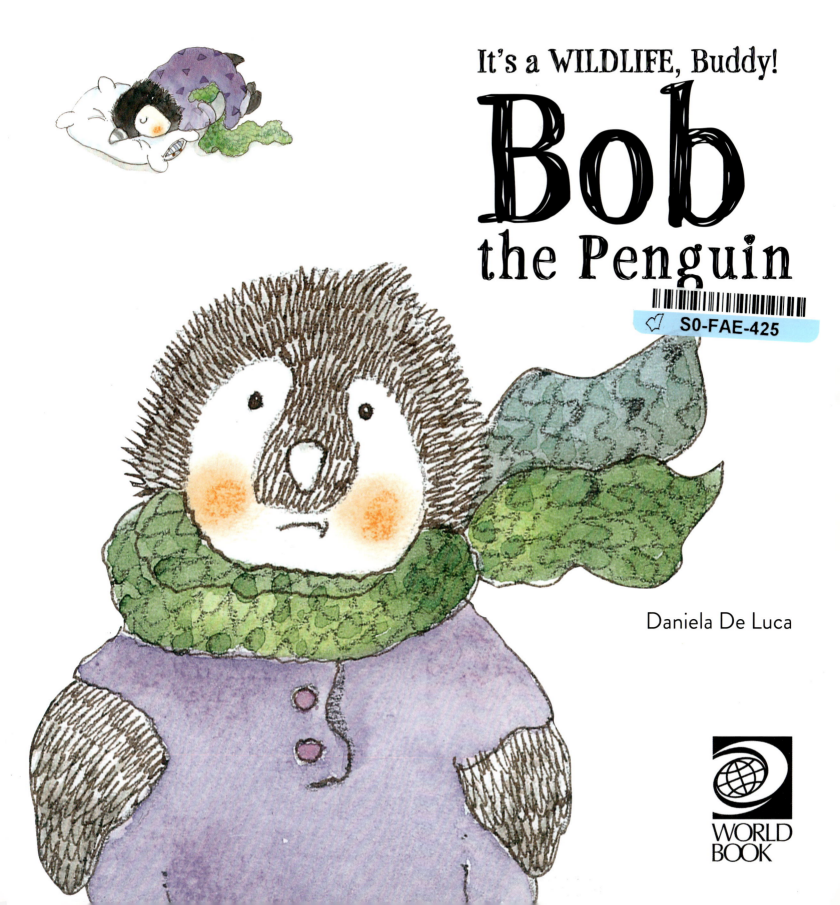

It's a WILDLIFE, Buddy!

Bob
the Penguin

Daniela De Luca

WORLD BOOK

World Book, Inc.
180 North LaSalle Street
Suite 900
Chicago, Illinois 60601
USA

For school and library sales, please phone
1-800-975-3250 (United States)
or 1-800-837-5365 (Canada).

www.worldbook.com

LIBRARY OF CONGRESS
CATALOGING-IN-PUBLICATION DATA
HAS BEEN APPLIED FOR.

Copyright © 2017 by Nextquisite Ltd, London
Publishers: Anne McRae, Marco Nardi
www.nextquisite.com

All illustrations by Daniela De Luca
Texts: Daniela De Luca, Anne McRae, Neil Morris
Editing: Anne McRae, Vicky Egan, Neil Morris
Graphic Design: Marco Nardi
Layout: Marco Nardi, Rebecca Milner

This edition edited and revised by World Book, Inc.
by permission of Nextquisite Ltd.

ISBN: 978-0-7166-3519-2 (set), 978-0-7166-3527-7 (Bob the Penguin)

Printed and bound in China
1st printing March 2017

SOUTHERN OCEAN

ANTARCTICA

SOUTH
POLE

SOUTHERN OCEAN

ARE PENGUINS REALLY BIRDS?

Yes, they certainly are birds. Their body is covered with feathers, but they cannot fly. All the different kinds of penguins live near the cold **coasts** of southern oceans.

EVERY FALL THE EMPEROR PENGUINS set off south on the long journey to their meeting place near the **South Pole**. They march along day after day across the ice and snow. Alfred has been on this march many times, but this year he finds it more tiring than ever. "I'm getting too old for this," he says, but soon he's on the move again.

At last they arrive at the meeting place, and the penguin party is soon in full swing. The penguins sip icy seawater from fancy glasses. They eat bits of fish from the ends of tiny icicles. Alfred sees a very special friend of his in the crowd.

WHY DO EMPEROR PENGUINS WALK SO FAR?

They may travel more than 60 miles (100 km) across the ice to reach their breeding grounds. Once there, female and male penguins join up to mate and start a family together.

FLORA IS WEARING a purple shawl, and Alfred thinks she looks
even prettier than he remembers from last year. He is glad
to spot her in the crowd! He calls out happily, hoping that
Flora hasn't forgotten his voice.

DO EMPEROR PENGUINS BUILD A NEST?

No, they keep their egg warm in a different way.
After she lays the egg, the female passes it to the
male, who holds it on his feet under a fold of skin.
This space is called a brood pouch. Then the female
can go off to feed. When the egg has hatched, the
male passes the chick back to his mate. The male
and female take turns caring for the chick so each
parent has time to feed.

ALFRED POLITELY BOWS TO FLORA. He nods his handsome head to catch her eye. At first Flora looks the other way, but then she bows too and the couple waddle off together. Alfred is pleased that Flora has chosen him to be her mate. Soon Flora will lay an egg, and later the proud parents will have an emperor penguin chick!

WHEN THE CHICK HAS HATCHED from the egg, Alfred and Flora have a boy. The parents decide to call their son Bob. Flora and Alfred take turns looking after their chick. They both get very tired and need to walk a long way to the coast to catch some fish to eat. They take turns doing that, too, so that they both keep their strength up.

HOW MANY EGGS DOES AN EMPEROR PENGUIN LAY?

A female emperor penguin lays just one egg each year, in May or June. The egg is about 5 inches (13 cm) long. Emperor penguins live for up to 20 years in the wild.

HOW DO PENGUIN CHICKS KEEP WARM?

Chicks have thick, fluffy **down** feathers that keep them warm in the early weeks. At about seven weeks they lose their gray down and grow adult feathers.

POOR LITTLE BOB feels very cold. His mother says this is quite a problem, because they live in the coldest part of the world!

BUT FLORA FEELS SORRY for her chick and gives him a blanket. When he still is cold, she wonders what to do. Then she has a brilliant idea!

FLORA DECIDES TO KNIT a warm set of clothes for little Bob. First she makes him soft overalls. Then she knits him a long, thick scarf. Bob helps his mother so she'll finish the scarf more quickly.

Now BOB is the warmest chick in the whole **colony**!

HOW DO PENGUINS FEED THEIR CHICKS?

Emperor parents take turns to go off and catch fish and other sea creatures for food. They eat some themselves and store the rest in their crop, a pouch in the throat. Later, they can bring some of this food up into their throat and feed it to the chick.

HOW BIG ARE EMPEROR PENGUINS?

Emperor chicks are small, but they grow into the biggest penguins of all. As adults emperors reach a height of about 3 feet (1 m) and weigh as much as 100 pounds (45 kg).

FLORA HAD ANOTHER REASON for knitting Bob's bright green scarf.
She thought it would help her find him in the crowded colony.
There's lots going on today. But where is Bob?

Ah, THERE'S BOB, in the playground. Everyone seems to be having fun, but why is Bob hiding under the slide?

His parents have shown Bob all around the colony. But he is a very shy little penguin, and he hasn't made any friends yet.

Bob is hiding as usual when an icy snowstorm blows up. All the penguin parents have gone fishing, so the chicks huddle together to keep warm. But Bob is late joining the group and he's stuck at the edge of the crowd, where it's freezing. It's lucky he is wearing his green scarf.

HOW CAN FEATHERS KEEP PENGUINS WARM?

Penguins have many short feathers that make up a dense, or thick, waterproof coat. The feathers lie one on top of another, overlapping like roof tiles. Penguins have more feathers than most birds and grow new ones every year.

DO PENGUINS REALLY HUDDLE TOGETHER?

Emperor penguins do. They huddle, or crowd together, to escape the cold blowing wind and stay warm. They take turns standing on the outside so each one has time to warm up near the center.

19

ONCE THE SNOWSTORM is over, Bob feels a bit warmer. He made some friends in the huddle, and now he has fun playing games with them. But Bob's not used to games. He goes too near the edge of an ice cliff and suddenly finds himself heading beak-first into the sea!

ARE PENGUINS GOOD SWIMMERS?

Yes, they are fast, skillful swimmers. They can move as fast as 10 miles (16 kilometers) per hour. They use their flippers to push themselves and their feet to steer. Penguins can dive as deep as 2,000 feet (600 meters) and have good underwater vision.

Bob MAKES A BIG SPLASH when he hits the water. He has never tried to swim before, so he'll have to learn fast! The other penguins fear the worst when they see a big leopard seal heading straight for Bob. "That chick will make a tasty snack," the leopard seal thinks. Who can save Bob now?

HOW MANY PENGUINS ARE THERE IN A COLONY?

There may be as many as 20,000 pairs of birds in an emperor penguin colony. A breeding colony, where males and females find mates, is called a rookery.

23

BOB IS VERY LUCKY! The petrel
who was resting on the
icy cliff is faster than the
leopard seal. The big bird
swoops down and pulls Bob
from the sea.

DO ANY BIRDS ATTACK PENGUINS?

The bird called a skua (right), pronounced SKYOO uh, will try to snatch emperor penguin chicks, and it has even been known to attack adult penguins. As its name says, the South Polar skua flies all the way to the South Pole.

WHICH ANIMALS DO LEOPARD SEALS HUNT?

Leopard seals live around the edge of large areas of frozen seawater called pack ice. There they can hunt and catch penguins, smaller seals, fish, and squid.

POOR LITTLE BOB is exhausted, but all the adults are relieved that he is safe and well.

25

Now THAT IT'S SUMMER again, the penguins, seals, gulls, and other animals enjoy the sunshine at the Antarctic coast. Bob is warm at last, and his mother is relaxed and happy. In a few months it will be time for the long march south. But that's the last thing on the penguins' mind on this sunny day!

26

FIORDLAND PENGUIN

DID YOU KNOW?

Bob is an emperor penguin. This is just one of many species, or different kinds, of penguin. On this page you can see five other kinds. Which do you think is the smallest penguin? Yes, it's the little penguin!

EMPEROR PENGUIN AND CHICK

BOB

ADÉLIE PENGUIN

AFRICAN PENGUIN

LITTLE PENGUIN

CHINSTRAP PENGUIN

ARE THERE OTHER BIRDS THAT DO NOT FLY?

Yes, there are quite a few flightless birds, and you can see some of them on this page. Ostriches live in Africa, the emu in Australia, and the rhea in South America. The cassowary is from New Guinea. The kakapo, kiwi, and takahe live in New Zealand. Kiwi has become a nickname for a New Zealander.

OSTRICH

CASSOWARY

EMU

RHEA

TAKAHE

KAKAPO

KIWI

PETREL

Here is Bob with some of his friends. They all live in the Antarctic region, at the bottom of the world near the South Pole. Which of Bob's friends have you learned about?

BOB

LEOPARD SEAL

EMPEROR PENGUIN

WEDDELL SEAL AND PUP

FIORDLAND PENGUIN

Blue whale

Albatross

Adélie penguin

Killer whale

Elephant seal

(Animals not shown to scale.)

Glossary

Terms defined in this glossary are in type that **looks like this** (bold type) on their first appearance on any two facing pages (a spread).

coast - the land along the sea; the seashore

colony - a group of animals of the same kind, living and growing together

down - soft feathers

South Pole - a term for an invisible point on the surface of the Antarctic region where all Earth's lines of longitude meet. Lines of longitude mark distances east and west on Earth's surface.

Note to the Grown-Ups: Each "It's a Wildlife, Buddy!" book combines a whimsical narrative and factual background information to help children learn a little life lesson and a few things about some animals with which we share the world. We have the animal characters say and do things that are not possible for them in the wild to create stories that can appeal to children and that they can relate to. The stories can help children think about making friends, growing up, and other important parts of their lives. The fanciful stories are balanced by basic facts about the animals' lives and behaviors in nature. This combination creates a satisfying and informing reading experience whether an adult is reading to a child or a child is reading on his or her own.